MORE PRAISE FOR TAYLOR MALI

The stars were aligned that night in the exact middle of the 60's when Taylor Mali came into this world. He is doing what he was born to do: a poet-warrior carrying into the present age all that youthful Promethean rebellion and titanic creative energy, now radically fused with the crucial discipline and authority of the true teacher. "He who cannot obey himself will be commanded," said Nietzsche, and thus too speaks Taylor Mali, while laughing.

—Richard Tarnas, Professor of Philosophy and Cultural History at the California Institute of Integral Studies, author of *The Passion of the Western Mind* and *Cosmos and Psyche*

Taylor Mali captures in his irresistible persona and highly engaging poetry the experience of the independent school teacher that he once was: part inspiration, part nag, part coach and friend, part disciplinarian. Kids love him and his poetry…and so do adults, a combination of approbation that is unusual in today's world.

—Patrick F. Bassett, President, National Association of Independent Schools

THE LAST TIME AS WE ARE

BY TAYLOR MALI

A Write Bloody Book
Nashville. Los Angeles. USA

The Last Time As We Are
by Taylor Mali

Write Bloody Publishing ©2009.
1ˢᵗ printing.
Printed in NASHVILLE, TN USA

The Last Time As We Are Copyright 2009. All Rights Reserved.

Published by Write Bloody Publishing.

Printed in Tennessee, USA.

Cover Designed by Joshua Grieve
Interior Layout by Lea C. Deschenes
Type set in Helvetica Neue and Bell MT
Edited by Derrick Brown, shea M gauer, Saadia Byram, Michael Sarnowski
Proofread by Jennifer Roach

To contact the author, send an email to writebloody@gmail.com

WRITE BLOODY PUBLISHING
NASHVILLE, TN

For Marie-Elizabeth,
standing in the center of the fire

THE LAST TIME AS WE ARE

Foreword 13

The Call to What We Know 15

Life Work 17
    The Moon Exactly How It Is Tonight 19
    The Practice of the Broom 20
    Tuesday Nights Outside the Church of Gustavus Adolphus 22
    Silver-lined Heart 23
    The Egyptian Death Position 26
    We Could Live Here 28
    Necessary Fuel 30
    Whosoever has dreamt of secret basements 31
    When the Monks Came to Chant at Kripalu 32
    The Ocean Inside 33
    The Basic Paradox 35
    Thrift Shop Chic 36
    The Last Postcard 38
    Bats Startled Into Flight 39
    Shock and Awe 40
    Pink Slip 41
    A Dog Named Bodhisattva 42
    Ars Poetica 45
    When the Activity of the Day Is Done 47
    What Bread to Eat 48

Class Work 51
    Miracle Workers 53
    The Mysteries of the Jack and Spare 56
    Who I Teach is Also What 57

Memorize This Sentence for Casual Use in Conversation 59
What You Need to Teach 60
There's No They're Their 62
Barking in the Darking 63
When Does the Heart Rest? 65
Talking to an Identical Twin 67
Any Language, Much Less English 68
Pizza 70
The Penis Warriors 72
Virgin Ears 75
I'll Fight You for the Library 77
Tony Steinberg: Brave Seventh-Grade Viking Warrior 80

Homework 85
Love Hungry for Itself 87
The Missing Shepherd of Your Dreams 88
King Comforter 90
Starfish in the Middle of the Bed 92
Happiness Itself 93
The Space Long-term Love Requires 94
Four Ways We Love Each Other 95
The Blooming 97
The Thing Itself 98
Montreal 99
The Loving Kill 100
Reading Allowed 102
The Seven Deadly Kappas 104
The Last Time As We Are 105
As with a Marriage and Its Fire 106
Remember Me From Now 108

Study Questions 111

About the Author 115

Many thanks to: Cristin O'Keefe Aptowicz; my siblings and all their children; my godfather Edgar Koerner; father figures Galway Kinnell, Billy Collins, and Bob Holman; Jeffrey Kay and his XXL video camera; Sherry Marks and all the residents of the Brown Gardens Assisted Living Residence Hall; and everyone in the New York City spoken word community, especially Lynne Procope, Shappy, Sarah Kay, Rives, and above all my wife and best friend Marie-Elizabeth.

Print Acknowledgements

Many thanks to these journals which published the following poems, sometimes in slightly different form:

Barnwood: "When the Activity of the Day is Done" and "Montreal"

Cadillac Cicatrix: "The Last Time as We Are"

Imitation Fruit: "Talking to an Identical Twin"

The Nail 10: "Whosoever has dreamt of secret basements"

Naugatuck River Review: "The Seven Deadly Kappas"

O&S Volume 2 Issue 4: "Pink Slip," "The Basic Paradox," "Tuesday Nights Outside the Church of Gustavus Adolphus," and "King Comforter"

Paddlefish: "Thrift Shop Chic"

Pank 4: "The Last Postcard"

Tampa Review: "As With a Marriage and Its Fire"

Recording Acknowledgements

Audio or video versions of some of the poems in this book can be found, sometimes in slightly different form, on iTunes, YouTube, Audible.com, and on the following CDs and podcasts:

Indiefeed.com: "Reading Allowed" and "A Dog Named Bodhisattva"

Conviction: "Tony Steinberg: Brave Seventh-Grade Viking Warrior" and "Silver-lined Heart"

Icarus Airlines: "Miracle Workers," "Pizza," "Reading Allowed," "Thrift Shop Chic," "A Dog Named Bodhisattva," and "When Does the Heart Rest?"

Excellence in the Field of Awesomeness (Best of NYC-Urbana 2007-2008): "Love Hungry for Itself"

FOREWORD

If you love teaching so much, then how come you're not still doing it?

I used to hate getting this question after my readings. But it's a good one. My love for the art of teaching is palpable in my work, and my love for teachers themselves is manifest in everything I do. A poem I wrote over ten years ago, "What Teachers Make," has been sent around the world as inspirational cyber spam by well-meaning souls who wish only to remind teachers why they chose to walk the noble path they walk. That's fine with me. I'll choose anonymous inspiration over taking credit every time.

But the fact remains that I said goodbye to my last sixth-grade homeroom class in June of 2000 and haven't set foot in a school since except as a visiting writer or poet-in-residence. Oftentimes I'm just the ponytailed poet in mostly black from New York City brought in for the morning assembly. Last month, I flew to Nebraska and back in one day just for an afternoon reading. I belong to seven frequent flier programs, and these days I rarely see the same kids more than once. Make no mistake, I love what I do now—I make a living writing and performing poetry and teaching others how to do the same! Who knew you could do that?—but I miss what I used to do and the kind of difference it used to make.

Yet every time I have publically lamented from the stage that I am not still a teacher, someone has come up to me and told me that I am still teaching. That I have never stopped. After all, as the Roman poet Horace said over 2,000 years ago, the task of the poet is "to instruct or entertain," hopefully at the same time. How is that not also the task of the teacher? My work has inspired 308 people to enter the field of education. At this rate, I'll reach my goal of 1,000 in 2030 when I'm 65 years old and at the height of my game!

Could it be that I am more useful to the teaching profession outside the classroom than I was when I was in it? Perhaps. But I prefer to think that I simply have a different kind of classroom now. And by picking up this book and reading these poems, you've just entered that classroom. Welcome.

Taylor Mali
New York City
March 1, 2009

THE CALL TO WHAT WE KNOW

The last thing this world needs
is another poem about flowers,
the passing hours, or the demands of time,
written in language no one understands,
and doesn't rhyme.

         Every time I have turned
to words and found or heard a truth
I never knew I'd learned by heart,
it was always proof I was a part
of something bigger than myself,
a communion of dark moonlight
with night ground, or the union
of a kiss forgiving only this:
We the living delight in sound.

LIFE WORK

You teach best what you most need to learn.
—Richard David Bach

THE MOON EXACTLY HOW IT IS TONIGHT

When Mount Everest was measured in 1856
it was discovered to be 29,000 feet exactly.
But since no one would have believed the figure,

sounding as it does too much like something
rounded off, two extra feet were found,
invented out of thin air, the thinnest on earth,

and added to the mountain's top
to provide the appearance of precision.
Twenty-nine thousand and two.

So too, tonight, a cloud has passed
before the moon in such a way
that were I able to describe it

exactly how it is, no one would believe me.
Which is why I need two extra feet of moonlight,
or dark cloud, or to be fair, one foot of each.

THE PRACTICE OF THE BROOM

You must sweep
the same floor daily
to know how much
dust can gather in a day,
which is not a lot,
or the work a single
spider can accomplish
in the same time,
which is.

It must be swept,
the place kept clean.
More so, if possible,
than the day before.
Love comes from nothing,
as everything does,
which is to say, no one
ever knows its source
or where it goes.

I commit myself
to the practice
of the broom, the pen,
the heart inside
the body, knowing,
as with law

and every meditation,
the work is never done.
Nor would I want it so.

TUESDAY NIGHTS OUTSIDE THE CHURCH OF GUSTAVUS ADOLPHUS

An odd assortment of men
stands outside the church
(every Tuesday nights) smoking,
their common addiction
stronger than Jesus.

I want to ask what they come for
and whether they find it
but am afraid, perhaps,
that having once been told,
I will need it too.

SILVER-LINED HEART

I'm for reckless abandon
and spontaneous celebrations of nothing at all,
like the twin flutes I kept in the trunk of my car
in a box labeled *Emergency Champagne Glasses!*

Raise an unexpected glass to long, cold winters
and sweet, hot summers and the beautiful confusion
of the times in between.
To the unexpected drenching rain that leaves you soaking
wet and smiling breathless.

Here's to the soul-expanding power of the universally
optimistic simplicity of the beautiful.

See, things you hate, things you despise,
multinational corporations, and lies that politicians tell,
injustices that make you mad as hell,
that's all well and good.
And as far as writing poems goes,
I guess you should.
It just might be a poem that gets Mumia released,
brings an end to terrorism or peace in the Middle East.

But as far as what soothes me, what inspires and moves me,
honesty behooves me to tell you your rage doesn't move me.
See, like the darkest of clouds my heart has a silver lining,

which does not harken to the loudest whining,
but beats and stirs and grows ever more
when I learn of the things you're actually for.

That's why I'm for best friends, long drives, and smiles,
nothing but the sound of thinking for miles.
For the unconditional love of dogs:
may we learn the lessons of their love by heart.
For therapy when you need it,
and poetry when you need it.
And the wisdom to know the difference.

I'm for hard work, and homework,
and chapter tests, and cumulative exams,
and yearly science fairs, and pop quizzes
when you least expect them just to keep everybody honest.
For love and the fragile human heart:
may it always heal stronger than it was before.
For walks in the woods, and for the woods themselves,
by which I mean the trees. Definitely for the trees.
Window seats, and locally brewed beer,
and love letters written by hand with fountain pens:
I'm for all of these.

For Galway Kinnell, and Rufus Wainwright,
and Mos Def, and the Indigo Girls,
and getting closer to fine each and every day.

For the integrity it takes not to lightly suffer fools.
For God, and faith, and prayers, but not in public schools.

I'm for evolution more than revolution
unless you're offering some kind of solution.
Isn't that how we got the Consitution?

For charm and charisma and style
without being a self-important prig.
For chivalry and being a gentleman at the risk
of being called a male chauvinist pig.

I'm for crushes not acted upon, for admiration from afar,
for intense sessions of self-love,
especially if they make you a nicer person.

I'm for the courage it takes to volunteer,
to say "yes," "I believe in this," and "I will."
For the bright side, the glass half full, the silver lining,
and the optimists who consider darkness just a different
    kind of shining.

I'm for what can be achieved more than for
what I would want in an ideal world.
I'm for working every day to make the world a better place
and not complaining about how it isn't.

So don't waste my time and your curses on verses
about what you are against, despise, and abhor.
Tell me what inspires you, what fulfills and fires you.
Put your goddamn pen to paper and tell me what you're for!

THE EGYPTIAN DEATH POSITION

Rarely at night was falling asleep
ever a problem for me, but still,
nights when the next day was bigger than usual,
I lay in the valley of my horsehair mattress
listening to the traffic on Park Avenue
and began a strange ritual.

On my back, I straightened myself out completely,
head cocked needed uncocking, hips unshifted,
unakimboed elbows, knees unbent, and fingers.
Nothing touched nothing, and I worked
at total stillness until it seemed that even breathing
required more effort than I wanted to spend.
I didn't try to die, but if I could have
stopped my heart I might have tried.

It was The Egyptian Death Position,
even though I never said the words
out loud, even to myself, until now.
I lay there unmoving and thought of nothing:
not the cars, my brother sleeping in the next bed over,
my parents in the next room loving each other,
my sisters away at boarding school,
Elma dreaming of Jamaica in the maid's room,
the red front door, our dog, the red rug
in the giant playroom where I kissed the lips

of the woman I would marry twenty-five years later.
Didn't think about sex, or even girls—their hair,
and their lips, their beautiful eyes, and the mystery
of what they don't have—ancient history, the pyramids,
the pharaohs, the mummy I was imitating, even
the Temple of Dendur recently brought over from Egypt
block by block and reassembled in the Metropolitan Museum
of Art in a special wing of mostly glass so that even at night
you could see it with the lights on inside.

I lay in my bed like that, like the stones of a temple,
heavy resting stones so far away from their home.

WE COULD LIVE HERE

In a tree house,
it may be the first time
you bring food, pull up the rope ladder,
and think you have everything you need;
in a closet, it could be when you lay down the blanket
or sneak in a radio, lock the door from the inside
and stick glow-in-the-dark stars on the ceiling;
and in a shed, or an abandoned outbuilding,
it might be finally sweeping the floor,
cracking a white tablecloth over an upturned crate;
but at some point during the preparation
of a secret space, at some critical mass
of coziness, someone will eventually say,
We could live here!

It doesn't matter where you are.
We could live here.
It doesn't matter who you are.

You could be the happiest kid in the world
living in a beautiful house with loving parents
who give you everything you need
(and most of what you want)
but start cleaning out the garage
with all its cobwebs and piles
of hazardous waste in the corner—
get the attic swept and aired out

and sooner or later someone will say,
We could live here!

Now imagine a senior citizen residence center
where a thirty-seven-year-old poet comes once a month
to read poetry to a wrinkled but adoring clutch
of old ladies who sometimes nod off but sometimes
say things like, *Your words make me feel anointed!*
Or, when they're feeling fresh, *You can leave
your slippers under my bed anytime!*

And what's that worth?
I don't think things have a grand scheme,
but if they did, what would that be worth
in the grand scheme of things?
Is that even one push of the broom?
Do any of America's stars glow
in the dark like they do on the ceiling
of the linen closet of my childhood?
Can you bring about peace in the world
by helping old ladies across the street?
Does it even register in the world's tree house?

God, in addition to the serenity, the courage, and the wisdom
I ask for every day, grant me the knowledge
that what I do can make a difference,
that the words of poets can be brooms and rope ladders,
glow-in-the-dark stars, and white tablecloths.
Please let me know that one day we will
look upon this planet we call home
and say *Hey, we could live here!*

NECESSARY FUEL

More than anything to burn, fire needs fuel,
and more than any fuel, it needs the air;
it must be there. The wisdom of the andiron
is the lift it gives the kindling wood, split
logs, which spit and cry with a colored flame.

Anyone who knows the tools of the fire—
the tongs and the shovel, the broom,
and the sharpened point of the poker—
knows it is the bellows that most can grow
the flame and make the burning blow.

So the best you can hope for is a busted crate—
think apples, or peaches, or a wine-stained case
with rusty nails, cracked slats, and splinters,
something barely capable of holding anything
now except its shape, and therefore the air,

which is all you need it to hold anyway,
and which never spills, even now upside down
with the bones of the fire built all around it
and on top, and everywhere but inside this box
of air, the necessary fuel, this burning box of fire.

WHOSOEVER HAS DREAMT
OF SECRET BASEMENTS

and the previously unknown places they go—
the new doorway and the ragged wet extension
to which it now opens like a mouth—
and the things that have gone on there,
and then woken in his own house to discover

he has no basement, was not punished as a child
so far as he remembers, or is, for lack of a better word,
happy, knows what it means to wonder at his life
as at a strange bird with bright wings and a head
the color of blood, its throat open, singing
for all the world a song he cannot hear.

WHEN THE MONKS CAME TO CHANT AT KRIPALU

so did the thunder. I had seen the lightning
in the distance, even prayed for rain.
And when the chant master raised his hand
so as to feel the song's rumble in his fingers,
and the thunder chose that moment to rip
a rainless clap, I wondered if it came to lend
its crackling tumble to his song.

Afterward, outside, still with no rain,
I saw him watching the lightning
and joined him. Holding my hand
like his, I did my best to sound
like thunder, and he smiled and pointed
to my throat, then to my heart.

I drove right home, straight into
the lightning, chanting in the car.
I sang as far into the thunder
as I could, from my throat
and lower, finally reaching
home the moment the rain came down.

THE OCEAN INSIDE
OR, WHY ONE TEACUP FELL, BUT NOT THE OTHER

The wind is strong. It's a choppy sea.
Most things upright are not stable.
But standing there in front of me
are two teacups on the galley table.

One red, one blue, standing tall,
on the table after breakfast in front of me,
until the ship lurches and the red cup falls,
a victim of the swell of the sea.

Why would one fall but not the other?
I ask as I reach out with one hand.
Why the red sister but not the blue brother?
Then grasping, I understand.

The blue, still upright and standing there,
has tea too hot to drink; it's full.
But the red one was empty (or full of air)
and so did not feel the ocean's pull

and sway (or rather did but would not
match that lurching with a similar motion).
The tea could do what the air could not:
mimic the rocking of the turbulent ocean.

No metaphors here, just this understanding:
Whenever you're traveling the ocean wide,
be like a teacup—if you want to stay standing—
at least partly full of the ocean inside.

THE BASIC PARADOX

Forget every lesson you've ever been taught.
The practice of grace becomes part of the grind.
You are the seeker and also the sought.

Burn all your bridges and the books you bought.
Those who can't see will be led by the blind.
Forget every lesson you've ever been taught.

You can't *think* your way free from a prison of thought.
What looks like the lifeline is part of the bind.
You are the seeker and also the sought.

Stop fighting the fires you've always fought;
never mind the chatter of the chattering mind.
Forget every lesson you've ever been taught.

The mind is the trap in which the mind is caught.
What can be left must be left behind.
You are the seeker and also the sought.

The truth is that which cannot be forgot
(what never was lost is the hardest to find).
Forget every lesson you've ever been taught.
You are the seeker and also the sought.

THRIFT SHOP CHIC

Whenever I'm in Paris, before I leave,
I buy cheap bottles of French red wine
to bring back home with me.

So that later I can bring one out
with a flourish—*I brought this back
from France!*—and we can relish

how wonderfully good even bad wine
can be—so dark and continental—
if it happens to come from France.

I used to tell this story as an example
of my sense of Thrift Shop Chic
until you called me an ass

and pointed out that anyone
who begins a story with the words
Whenever I'm in Paris

should not presume to speak
on the topic of Thrift Shop Chic
with any kind of authority.

But I do love thrift shops. As did you.
In fact, it was the only thing
we ever had in common.

Except you liked them for the gems
you might find there, and I for all
they would take off my hands.

THE LAST POSTCARD

Once, before a trip I took to Europe,
I rewrote my will, sure that I would die
before returning. I almost didn't pack
a bag, but was glad I did,
though I forgot a change of socks.

So I survived the flight here, I thought,
So what? Now I will be beaten by skinheads
in Munich, or be struck by a gorgeous,
elegantly engineered Italian car.

The day before I was to return,
I knew, I just knew, that my plane home
would never land, but would instead
rain down fire all over Iceland.
So I bought all the postcards
in the corner store and wrote
to everyone I knew the last
postcard they would ever receive
from me, all of them doleful
and divinatory like the sound
of a train on time. I wrote,

When you read this,
know that I am happy
now, at the moment of writing.
Life is beautiful,
even with the rain.

BATS STARTLED INTO FLIGHT

The story this morning of an accidental hanging
that claimed the life of a popular boy
in the local high school has me at once
sliding down the fire pole my father fixed
to the floor and ceiling of the barn
with a noose of baling wire around my neck—
the other end wrapped high and tight
to the center beam—on a dare
from Paddy Crossman, one summer slip
away from a purple jerking pendulum of kicks
and creaking and Paddy's scream
that would have sent a thousand bats
tearing from the rafters out the barn doors
as he ran to get help every single night of his life.

SHOCK AND AWE

The greater the power, the greater the desire
of patriots and fools to see that power used.

Once upon a time I bought a gun, just in case
I ever found myself on a dark street.
But soon I started looking for trouble,
whistling as though calling for a dog.

So please forgive those of us who wished
when the hurricane hit—downgraded
from Category 5 to 1 but still strong enough
to breach, drown, and rent levies,
innocents, and the already overstretched
trust of the forever battered; those of us
who wished—wished without consequence—
that it had stayed as strong as it once was
to see what greater damage might be done.

PINK SLIP

A woman enters the train at Grand Central
and chooses not to take one of the empty seats,
as if doing so, relaxing the body even that tiny bit,
would invite the tears that have started to well
in her pretty eyes to fall.

It is 10:30 on a Friday morning, and I ask her
if everything is all right, knowing two things:
no one expects to be seen in this desperate city,
and when they are, when a stranger stops to ask
if you are okay, you never are and burst into tears.

She has just been laid off. Without warning.
Was told to clear out her desk, except for the phone,
which they had already taken. So she has spoken
to no one. And doesn't know what she would say
anyway. Or what she will do now.

Two men offer her napkins, the sight of a woman
in tears being what it is to all men. And I say
the only thing there is to say, the only thing
I can think of that might help. Which is nothing.

A DOG NAMED BODHISATTVA

There's a big dog running for all he's worth
and his feet hardly seem to touch the earth.
And his name is Bodhisattva, and he has four legs.

And Bodhisattva lives in a part of Oakland, California,
popular with Democrats and lesbians. Democratic lesbians
overrun the coffee shops and bars. Republican lesbians live
    elsewhere—
like Mars. And Bodhisattva runs like a happy fool
scaring the girls of the corner public school
who scream, "Oh my God! It's a dog!"
but who cried the day he almost died, struck
by some speeding idiot in a pickup truck.

Bodhisattva recovered except for one leg
in the front, which atrophied so if you asked him to beg
he'd sit and could only offer the one that didn't work.
As if to say, "Please, take this from me. It hurts."
But his owner didn't know that's what he was doing
and woke up one night to find Bodhisattva chewing
on the withering limb in the living room alone,
drunk on the taste of his own blood, biting down to the bone
as though by pain simply trying to prove it
still existed, or maybe just to remove it.

There's a big dog running for all he's worth

and his feet hardly seem to touch the earth.
And his name is Bodhisattva, and he has three legs.

That's right, they went to the vet and had the leg chopped off,
cremated, with the ashes kept in an urn aloft
on the mantelpiece over the fireplace
and when Bodhisattva came near that space,
he'd sit, and though you couldn't see it, he'd beg,
offering his missing limb to thc ashcs of his missing leg.

And just so you know, when Bodhisattva peed,
he still peed like a boy dog, there was no nccd
to squat likc a girl dog in the middle of the street.
He lifted his leg and touched it to the tree,
or the hydrant, or lamppost, or side of a picnic table:
he made three points of contact, and therefore kept stable.
To the girl doggies, he'd say, "What you looking at, bitch?"

And he still scared the girls at the corner public school,
a three-legged dog being scarier as a rule
than a regular four-legged one, more extreme.
"Oh my God! It's a three-legged dog!" they'd scream.

And so it went as many years passed
Bodhisattva scaring the girls and running fast
past the houses of the lesbians and Democrats
(who, in general, favor small dogs and cats).

But there came a day when Bodhisattva couldn't run outside.
And soon after came the day when Bodhisattva died.

His owner had him cremated, and then to ease his soul again
he added the ashes from the missing leg to make
    Bodhisattva whole again.

On the streets of Oakland late at night
some people swear they've seen the strangest sight:
A big dog running for all he's worth
and his feet hardly seem to touch the earth.
And his name is Bodhisattva, and he has four legs.

ARS POETICA

*To circumscribe poetry by a definition will
only show the narrowness of the definer.*
—Samuel Johnson

Anyone who thinks he knows poetry's definition
certainly *doesn't* know it.
'Cause the truth is there are as many definitions
as there are people who call themselves poets.

It's what oft' was thought but ne'er so well expressed;
the best words in the order that's also best;
A prayer to the otherwise unprayable.
That which is left when all else has ended;
the celebration of things only vaguely apprehended:
the art of saying the unsayable.

It's a human expression of life's beautifully complex and
        deadly futility.
Or the spontaneous overflow of powerful feelings
        recollected in times of tranquility.

That was Wordsworth, and for what it's worth
he came close to explaining what words can be worth.
Which is to say, you could do worse.
You test it on the pulse. It's jazz, the devil's wine, with
        extra sizzle.

All poetry is man's rebellion against being what he izzle.
For shizzle. It's the rhythmical creation of beauty in words.
What ideas would be if they didn't fly like birds.

A kind of literary mirror, a way to make things clearer.
Poetry is both the substance abused as well as the key to recovery.
A poem itself is therefore a kind of literate act of discovery.

I'm not saying I understand it. It's a mystery.
Plato was right when he said poetry is nearer vital truth
    than history.
That's Truth with a capital T. Not the facts, but the Truth
    as you know it.
That's one of the most appealing aspects there is to being a poet.
You can rewrite history to make yourself sound smarter
    than you actually are.
Recast the night sky of your own life to constellate
    yourself as a star.

We are the small gods of our own poems. We fix what
    cannot otherwise be fixed.
We are what is lost in translation, the clear explanation of
    feelings that are mixed.
Just as life would be a tragedy if it weren't so goddamn comical.
Poetry is a lot like prose but somehow more economical.

WHEN THE ACTIVITY OF THE DAY IS DONE

When you are showered and waiting
for dinner, maybe lying in a hammock
with a sweating glass of something
on the stump, reading, or listening
to a dog barking by the river's edge,
you might think that's the ideal time
to write a poem about the darkening day.

But you'd be wrong.

Because you're tired, and hungry,
and slung between two trees;
the erratic creaking back and forth
is all the music this moment needs.
The necessary edge is the river's edge;
and that little bit of dark insistence,
the distant, barking dog.

WHAT BREAD TO EAT

I don't want to tell you what you already know
so I won't tell you you're going to die.
Even so, there was a time
when such a revelation
would have felt a curse—
my mother told me not to cry,
that she, not I, would be the first
to die, which only made things worse.

And someone here will be the next to die.
This, too, must come as no surprise.
But this isn't a poem about the death
of that person—the next in this room to die—
this is about something else instead: the very last
one of us here to join the dead.

He or she who outlives the rest.

When that day comes—and may it take its time!—
by then who will care or even know we all once met,
gathered to share stories, rhymes, wine, and bread?
The rest of us all dead, except you:
the last one to go. When that day comes
who then will know?

I say *we* will.

We will be waiting for you in that other place
to do what we are doing now, face to face,
with whatever wine the dead have to drink,
what bread to eat. We will greet you and say,

Welcome. Come and eat.
And take, at last, your empty seat.

CLASS WORK

*Education is not about the filling of a bucket,
but the lighting of a fire.*

—William Butler Yeats

MIRACLE WORKERS

Sunday nights I lie awake—as all teachers do—
and wait for sleep to come as though sleep
were the last student in my class to arrive.
My grading is done, my lesson plans are in order,
and still sleep wanders the hallways like Lower School music.
I'm a teacher and that's what we do.

Like a builder builds, or a sculptor sculpts,
a preacher preaches, and a teacher teaches.
We are experts in the art of explanation:
we know the difference between the questions
to answer and the questions to ask.

"That's an excellent question. What do you think?"

If two boys are fighting, I break it up.
But if two girls are fighting, I wait until it's over
and then I drag what's left to the nurse's office.
I'm not your mother, or your father,
or your jailer, or your torturer,
or your biggest fan in the whole wide world
(even if sometimes I am all of these things);
I know you can do these things I make you do.
That's why I make you do them.
I'm a teacher and that's what we do.

Once, in a restaurant, when the waitress asked,
"Can I bring you anything else?"
And I said, "No thank you, just the check please,"
and she said, "How about a look at the dessert menu?"
I knew I had become a teacher when I said:
"What did I just say?
Please don't make me repeat myself!"

In the quiet hours of the dawn I write
my assignment sheets and print them
without spell checking them. Because I'm a teacher,
and teachers don't make spelling mistakes, do they?
So yes, as a matter of fact, the new School Dress Cod
will apply to all members of the 5th, 6th, and 78th grades;
and if you need an extension on your essays
examining The Pubic Wars from a hysterical perspective
you may have only until January 331st.
I trust that won't be a problem for anyone?

I like to lecture on love and speak on responsibility.
I hold forth on humility, compassion, eloquence, and charity.
At the drop of a hat, I will talk about honor, and integrity,
and the importance of telling the truth always.
And when my students ask,
"Are we going to be responsible for this?"
I say, "If not you, then who?
You think my generation will be responsible?
We're the ones who got you into this mess,
now you are our only hope."
And when they say, "What we meant, Mr. Mali,

is, are we going to be tested on this?"
I say, "EVERY SINGLE DAY OF YOUR LIVES!"

Once, I put a pencil on the desk of a student
who was digging in her backpack for a pencil.
But she didn't see me do it.
So when I walked to the other side of the classroom
and she raised her hand, still not seeing the pencil,
and said, "Mr. Mali, could I borrow a pencil?"
I intoned, "You already possess everything you require to succeed.
Including a pencil. Shazzam!"
For a moment, she *still* did not see the pencil, but said,
"You are definitely the weirdest teacher I have ever—
Oh my God! You're a miracle worker! How did you do that?"

And I wanted to say, "All I did was give you what I knew
        you needed
before you knew you needed it. So thank you for the compliment,
but education is the miracle, I'm just the worker.
I'm a teacher and that's what we do."

THE MYSTERIES OF THE JACK AND SPARE

Christine's first driving lesson was How To Change a Tire.
Her father was her teacher, the driveway her classroom.
And several times after that, the mysteries of the jack
and spare were revealed, until the day she turned sixteen

and got her driver's license, at which point her dad bought
a fifth tire, full-size, and lay down the law: *For the next year,*
until you are seventeen, every time you want to borrow the car
you must first replace one of the tires with the fifth tire.

There were times she was late, when she begged him
to let her skip the practice, but he refused every time.
For a year, she showed up everywhere with dirty hands,
cursing her goddamn dad, whom she did not know

how much she loved, until years later, on a date
with a boy who, she was disgusted to learn, had no idea
how to change a tire or treat a woman. So she dumped him
in nine minutes. Flat.

WHO I TEACH IS ALSO *WHAT*

Some ancient civilizations were denied
the land to grow their food and so relied
on trade or made their living from the sea.
Others raised great temples, cities of mud
and stone, or lived on mountaintops alone.
The same is true with the children I teach.

It's never a mystery teaching Ancient History
who is Egypt and who is Rome, which loner
in the corner thinks himself an island nation,
and which countries in Grade 6 civilization
have discovered iron weapons and survive
through fighting, as opposed to developing
an alphabet and therefore a system of writing.

And so it is with every subject:
Who I teach is *what* I teach.

By the time they reach my English class
it is not students that I teach but all
the different parts of speech, the adjectives
flying around the room describing everything,
like butterflies with beautiful wings,
while the nouns would rather speak of things.
The verbs all huddle together in a bunch,
shaking and jiggling, hungry for lunch.

Lastly in math, every student is a number, the girls,
in general, even, while the boys are mostly odd.
But the odd boy can be even, and even a girl
can be odd, like serious Daria with her thousand
tiny paper cranes, who lives with her aunt
and stays to herself most of the time, indivisible
by anything except herself and one, being
therefore prime.

MEMORIZE THIS SENTENCE
FOR CASUAL USE IN CONVERSATION

If you were the type of person who could,
without the slightest hesitation,
open your mouth and utter forth one beautiful sentence
with a syntax as easy to follow as a mile of twine
leading out of a complex maze,
then you might enjoy cultivating the idea
that eloquence is a quality that cannot be acquired,
that you are either born with the effortless ability
to produce fully formed thoughts as though crafted and delivered
to the tip of your tongue by God, or else you must resign yourself
to a life of little more than grunts;

but if, like me, you are one who labors over every word
and turn of phrase, who does not trust he can express
what he believes—or even know what he believes—
until first he has ground each word against each other
to see what crumbles and falls away
and what in the breaking may get even deadly sharper,
then you know that you do not betray the craft of writing
when sometimes you part the curtain to reveal the awkward gears,
the sputtering false starts and poorly chosen
ejaculations
that may first have burst forth
and threatened to hijack, disguise, or rip
the very guts out of your greatest truth,
of which in desperate need the world no doubt is.

WHAT YOU NEED TO TEACH

Ministers and rabbis and all the other caretakers and tour guides
of our souls have to listen to secrets and know how to keep
    them by heart.
And they show us what is sacred and what within ourselves
we should encourage. So if you don't feel qualified to be trusted
with that kind of responsibility, don't become a teacher.

And lawyers have to know the law to the letter, which
    means knowing
where it breaks and where it merely bends.
But they must have their clients' best interests at heart.
So if you can't make tough judgment calls,
don't think you can teach children.

And hostage negotiators have to be ready at all times to defuse
tense and dangerous situations. They weigh demands and
    expectations
and make sure nobody gets hurt. So don't walk into a classroom
if you're not prepared.

Teaching is about fixing flats and fine-tuning engines;
it's about hooking up cables, and providing access for everyone.
Sure, sometimes there are rabbits that must be pulled out of hats,
but there is bread that needs baking and meals
that have to make it to the table on time.

It's more than making sure every package gets delivered to the right kid. It's watching over the investments that children make and making sure that they are sound.

Don't teach if you can't administer justice, or lay strong
    foundations
in the earth to build upon. You will be called upon to sing
    and dance
and laugh until tears run through your veins like blood.
Expect there to be emergencies every day, so do not teach unless your hands have been scrubbed clean and you are ready to roll up your sleeves and get them dirty.

THERE'S NO THEY'RE THEIR

Grammar Challenge: Write a sentence that uses "there," "their," and "they're."

The students are there
at school, but they're
teasing each other instead of doing their
grammar homework.

On the outside they may look like normal kids
at school, but even though they're there,
their minds are elsewhere.

Individually and outside of school
each one is kind and considerate, but
there they're their
own worst enemies.

BARKING IN THE DARKING

If Roberto says he wants to be a veterinarian,
then you can say something like,
You are one sick animal, so that makes sense.

But if on the other hand
he says he wants to be a veterinarian in the U. S. Army,
you know, who cares for the pets of the soldiers—
except for the cats (he hates cats).
In fact, he would only work on dogs.
Let's face it, the United States
has the most advanced military in the world,
so they definitely have a vet who is a dog specialist.
And not just for the soldiers' pet dogs;
Roberto's practice would include combat dogs as well:
like bomb-sniffing dogs, scout dogs,
messenger dogs, search & rescue dogs
(with little barrels of whiskey like if you're cold)—
or maybe there are dogs who drive robots
that are too small for humans to get in
and maybe they get a paw stuck on a lever or something
and he'd have to put it in a splint?

In fact, there are probably top-secret programs
that involve dogs, like the Dogs in Space Program
(they probably call it Barking in the Darking
or something like that) and Roberto wants to do that:

Be the top-secret U. S. Army veterinarian
in charge of making sure that all dogs
in the Dogs in Space program are healthy and cleared for
    space travel.

If that's what Roberto tells you he wants to be
when he grows up, then there is only one thing to say.

Listen, Roberto. I have a free period now.
I was going to go to the faculty lounge to grade papers
and get ready for my next class.
But you have science right now,
and that is one class you, of all people,
cannot afford to miss.

WHEN DOES THE HEART REST?

Our science teacher asked the question,
and we laughed at the kid who said

When you sleep?

I raised my hand with what I was sure
was the correct answer—

When you die—

and then put it down quietly
when Angel got it right.

Between beats.

That didn't seem like enough time to me.
Still doesn't.

But it was Angel again in the schoolyard
standing up for the heart
when the older kid said the strongest muscle
in the human body was the jaw.

No, it is the heart.

The bully said we should have a contest—

between my jaw and your heart—
and we all laughed because it didn't seem like a fair fight.

And it still doesn't.
Because the heart rests and keeps working.
Between beats.
And my money is on Angel
and his heart,
not the bully and his jaw.

And anyone who thinks otherwise
can eat their heart out.

TALKING TO AN IDENTICAL TWIN

Before you spot the telltale clue—
the faint scar on the chin of one,
the slightly grayer eyes of the other—

when it still could be either twin
standing in front of you,
and you have no idea which,

it is not somehow both,
an amalgam of the two,
but neither. There is

the one; there is the other;
and then there is this third twin,
different from her sisters,

the one who always disappears
as soon as you recognize
who she is not.

ANY LANGUAGE, MUCH LESS ENGLISH

When I speak to people, I don't look them in the eyes;
I pick one—usually the left—and sink into it all the way
up to my ears, unblinking, and don't look away
no matter what they say. And I suppose that makes me
look somewhat intimidating.

And since by far the hardest part of listening
is keeping your own mouth shut, I try sometimes
just for fun, to breathe deeply through my nose
until my interlocutor is absolutely, entirely, totally finished.
And I've heard this makes me look angry.

And of course I'm a teacher, which apparently means
that I might, at any moment, whip out a red pen
and start exing your language in the air, circling every word
you mispronunciate and correcting your stultifyingly inelegant
syntax irregardless of the context in which you are speaking in!?
Oh, for crying out loud! You're killing me!

That could be part of the explanation as well.

But that being said, standing in front of me, speaking
face-to-face, some people seem to forget how to speak
any language, much less English.

So I'm here to tell you I don't speak in poetry when I talk.
I say "like," and "whatever," and "you know" without end.
I'm such a terrible speller that I once told a girlfriend
she was the passion of my lions.
"That said," "that being said," and "having said that"—
I use these phrases all the time to mean "I will stop talking
eventually, just not at any moment in the foreseeable future."

It's true, in public you need not only a vision,
but an eloquent way to convey it.
But in private I care more about what you say
than the words you choose to say it.

Having said that and that being said,
the message I want to impart is:
I don't care if your commas are in the right place
so long as I know that your heart is.

PIZZA
(for 134340)

Dear Pluto,

You will always be a planet in my solar system.

The International Astronomical Union
has demoted you, called you a dwarf planet,
and cast you in with the other icy bodies
of the Kuiper Belt.

But what do they know?

Who ever heard of the eight planets of the solar system?
My Very Educated Mother Just Served Us Nine?
That doesn't make any sense!
Without Pluto's Pizzas at the end
of the mnemonic device
children everywhere will go hungry.

We love the extremes.

The biggest and the smallest of everything
hold special places in our hearts.

Thus we were crushed when they took away Brontosaurus.[1]
They can't have you, too, Pluto!
What's next, Rhode Island?
The letter Q? February?
The penny?
It's just not right!

Give Pluto back to the planets.
Pluto lives!
Pluto rocks!

---

1   I hate to be the bearer of bad news—and this poem often is—but I assure you it's true. The 19th century paleontologist who named *Brontosaurus* mistakenly believed he had discovered a new species of sauropod when in fact he had only discovered a full-grown skeleton of an existing sauropod known as *Apatosaurus*. But before the mistake was discovered, the public had fallen in love with the idea of the massive *Brontosaurus*. However, since it is essentially a synonym for *Apatosaurus* the name *Brontosaurus* is no longer the preferred term for this particular species of sauropod.

THE PENIS WARRIORS

It's a Friday in September
and we're watching a video about gladiators.
A professor of antiquity
with an English accent is interviewed
and explains that the word gladiator
comes from the Latin word *gladius*,
which means sword.

"But it also meant penis.
So essentially everyone
gathered in the Coliseum
to watch these penis warriors
play with themselves."

Now at an all-boys school
in a classroom of thirteen-year-olds studying gladiators,
a sentence like that is guaranteed to stir a frenzy
that could only be rivaled
by the announcement that a real live girl
would be coming by later in the period
to model some of her favorite underwear.

"Gladiators are awesome!" says Milton,
who only months ago, when he was still a sixth grader,
warned the class while studying the Olympics
to look away whenever presented

with the marble buttocks of, say,
a naked statue of a discus thrower,
because "It will make you gay."
I do not know if Milton still believes this.
But apparently watching oily, muscle-bound gladiators
in leather loincloths battle with their penis/swords is not gay.
It's awesome.

Seventh grade is also the year
when most of the boys start taking Latin
so this new vocabulary word was corroborated
two periods later by Mrs. Elliott,
who had never taught at an all-boys school.
I say corroborated because she flatly denied
that *gladius* meant penis any more
than anything long and straight and hard meant penis.
"You wouldn't think I was talking about a penis
if I mentioned the words *shaft, rod,* or *staff,* would you?"
As I said, she had never taught at an all-boys school.

Jump forward about 700 years to another Friday,
and we're watching a video about Charlemagne.
It's the night of his wedding with his new wife,
the young princess of the Lombards,
and she rises from the bed
where she has left Charlemagne sleeping.
She wanders the bedroom admiring
the decorations and stops
in front of Charlemagne's suit of armor.
And as she reaches out to grasp

the handle of his sword, I hear Milton whisper,

"Chick digs the gladius."

And we all laugh because it's funny
if you speak Latin (or if, like me,
you just happened to be
in the right place at the right time).

VIRGIN EARS

The students want to know if I have any more dirty poems—
blue, perverted, scandalous: they want it all, hungry.
"Yes," I say, "but you're not old enough to hear them."
And then, just to see them writhe, I add,
"Because I use words you've never heard before."

One says, "We'll figure them out from context!"
Another says, "Wanna bet?"
A third starts listing all the swear words, curses, and body parts
she's ever heard of (some of which I have not)
like some sort of squalid litany to prove she's not that innocent.

There are things I've done that these kids have not,
I know. Like gone to college. And all they really want
is to hear a grown-up with a potty mouth, so my only hope
is to rely on undiscovered metaphor.

You think you know what it means to be dirty?

Have you ever blown the petals off someone's dandelion?
Do you know about chirping the chocolate chip nookie?
Have you ever swapped gargoyles, horizontally
(if you know what I mean!)?
What about performing the oral history of the Velveteen Rabbit
all while your tray table was in its full, upright and locked position?

I'm not sure you're ready for all the rainbows in my
    mouth, sister.
Brother, until you know the feeling of having your Rumsfeld,
your Ashcroft, or your Dick Cheney, you shouldn't run for office.
I like my George bushed three or four times a week.
Pig Latin, Kick the Can, and Naughty Smurf: these are the
    languages I speak.

They listen to me, entranced and amused, enthralled and confused.
And although that's pretty much what I remember of my teens,
I have no idea what I'm talking about, but they think they do.
It was not my intention to be disgusting, or flush
your cheeks and virgin ears. But, oops! I did it again.

I'LL FIGHT YOU FOR THE LIBRARY

(for Dr. Joseph D'Angelo, 5th grade English teacher, PhD, black belt, sensei)

1. To: Clarissa Lerner
Librarian

Dear Clarissa,

I understand that the periods I reserved in the library next week for my classes have been canceled. Just out of curiosity, who and/or what is more important than my classes' research needs?

2. To: Nancy Devlin
Secretary to Dr. Richard Blackstone, Dean of Instruction

Dear Nancy,

The librarian informs me that Dr. Blackstone has "reserved" the library for a "Facilities Utilization" meeting of the administration next week, and that all classes scheduled to meet in the library on that day must meet elsewhere. This is wrong. Academic instruction takes precedence over administrative meetings. Period. That Dr. Blackstone, the Dean of Instruction, would even CONSIDER canceling one class's library period in order to hold a meeting called "Facilities Utilization" is so obtuse, I am incapable of appreciating the irony in it.

3. To: Dr. Richard Blackstone
Dean of Instruction

Dear Dick,

With all due respect, I do not think you do understand my "frustration" or else you would not have used that word. See, I am not, in fact, frustrated. The correct word would be "outraged." I will not reschedule any of my classes' library periods for any administrative meeting, especially one that purports to be discussing the effective use of the school's facilities. I do not care if the library is the only place in the school big enough to accommodate your meeting. It is also the place in the school with books! And lastly, I would be the first to apologize for "editorializing through your secretary" if I thought that the statement "Academic instruction takes precedence over administrative meetings" were a matter of opinion, and not, in fact, a matter of fact. And not one that I thought I would have to explain to the Dean of Instruction. To conclude, if any of my classes are denied the use of the school's library to make room for an administrative meeting called "Facilities Utilization," then alert Joyce Santiago, the School Superintendent, to be ready to accept my resignation.

4. To: Dr. Joyce Santiago
School Superintendent

Dear Superintendent Santiago,

For thirty-five years, I have served the interests of my students, providing them with all the encouragement, guidance, resources, respect, and love they require to grow into productive, responsible, informed, and well-prepared members of the community. I do not take this responsibility lightly. I take it with all the nobility, grace, and gravitas of the teaching profession. So on behalf of my students and their parents, I thank you for finding another place for Dr. Blackstone to hold his meeting.

Sincerely,

Dr. Joseph D'Angelo, 5th grade English teacher, PhD, black belt, sensei

TONY STEINBERG:
BRAVE SEVENTH-GRADE VIKING WARRIOR

Have you ever seen a Viking ship made out of popsicle sticks
and balsa wood? Coils of brown thread for ropes,
sixteen oars made out of chopsticks, and a red and yellow sail
made from a ripped piece of a little baby brother's footie pajamas?

I have.

He died with his sword in his hand and so went straight to heaven.

The Vikings often buried their bravest warriors in ships.
Or set them adrift and on fire, a floating island of flames,
the soul of the brave warrior rising slowly with the smoke.
In order to understand life in Scandinavia in the Middle Ages,
you must understand the construction of the Viking ship.

So here's what I want the class to do:

I want you to build me a miniature Viking ship.
You have a month to complete this assignment.
You can use whatever materials you want,
but you must all work together.
Like warriors.

These are the projects that I'm known for as a history teacher.
Like the Greek Shield Project.

Or the Marshmallow Catapult Project.
Or the Medieval Castle of Chocolate Cake
(actually, that one was a disaster).
But there was the Egyptian Pyramid Project.
Have you ever seen a family of four
standing around a card table after dinner,
each one holding one triangular side
of a miniature cardboard Egyptian pyramid
until the glue finally dries?

I haven't either, but Mrs. Steinberg said it took 90 minutes,
and even with the little brother on one side saying,
"This is a stupid pyramid, Tony!
If I get Mr. Mali next year, my pyramid
will be designed in such a way that it will not necessitate
us standing here for ninety minutes while the glue dries!"
And Tony on the other side saying,
"Shut up! Shut up, you idiot!
If you let go before the glue dries
I will disembowel you with your Sony PlayStation!"
It was the best family time they'd spent together since Hanukkah.

He died with his sword in his hand and so went straight to heaven.

"Mr. Mali, if that's true,
that if you died with your sword in your hand
you would go straight to Valhalla,
then if you were, like, an old Viking
and you were about to die of old age,
could you keep your sword right by your bed

so if you ever felt, like, *I think I might die of old age!*
you could reach out and grab it?"

If I were a Viking God, I don't think I would fall for that.
But if I were an old Viking about to die of old age,
that's exactly what I would do. You're a genius.

He died with his sword in his hand and so went straight to heaven.

Tony Steinberg had been missing from school for six weeks
before we finally found out what was wrong.
And the twelve boys left whispered the name of the disease
as if you could catch it from saying it too loud.

We'd been warned. The Middle School Head had come to class
and said Tony was coming to school on Friday.
"But he's had a rough time.
The medication he's taking has made all his hair fall out.
So nobody stare, nobody point, nobody laugh."

I always said I liked teaching in a private school
because I could talk about God in the classroom
and not be breaking the law.
And I sure talk about God a lot in the classroom.
Yes, in history, of course, that's easy:
even the Egyptian Pyramid Project
is essentially a spiritual undertaking.
But how can you teach math and not believe in a God?

A God of perfect points and planes,
surrounded by right angles and arch angels of varying degrees.

Such a God would not give cancer to a seventh-grade boy.
Wouldn't make all his hair fall out from chemotherapy.
Totally bald in a jacket and tie on Friday morning—
and I don't just mean Tony Steinberg—
not one single boy in my class had hair that day;
the other twelve had all shaved their heads in solidarity.
Have you ever seen thirteen bald-headed seventh-grade boys,
all pointing at each other, all staring, all laughing?

I have.

And it's a beautiful sight.
Almost as striking as twelve boys
six weeks later—now with crew cuts—
on a Saturday morning,
standing outside the synagogue
with heads bowed, holding hands
and standing in a circle
around the smoldering remains
of a miniature Viking ship,
which they have set on fire,
the soul of the brave warrior
rising slowly with the smoke.

HOMEWORK

You never lose by loving. You always lose by holding back.

—Barbara De Angelis

LOVE HUNGRY FOR ITSELF

I love my wife, but I have never loved her
the way she deserves to be loved.
Nor has she loved me in the same way.

Once, we went to bed together
too tired to do anything but kiss,
which we did with our lips drifting.

But after the first dream, love hungry
for itself, we found ourselves making more
with great desire and the divinity of dark.

Leave me this great imperfect love
in which the body knows to seek
what the heart does not think it needs.

THE MISSING SHEPHERD OF YOUR DREAMS

I kissed you this morning
as you lay in the sweetest
final minutes,
and told you not to wake up,
that I would bring you coffee.

You mumbled thanks,
but just before falling
back into flannel added,
And a shepherd, please.

A shepherd?

Was this some kind of code
for milk and sugar?
Maybe sheep's milk?
Or a wool sweater?
I didn't think so.

And of course we already have a dog,
part shepherd no less, but she only looked at me
and blinked as if to say,
I have no idea what she's talking about.
And anyway, she asked you.

In the end I came to you empty-handed,
which is to say with only coffee.
Black. No sheep's milk, no wool sweater,
and certainly no shepherd.
And you seemed yourself unchanged.

But I wonder sometimes what scattered chaos
remained unflocked in your dreams;
what wolf of your unconscious, spying
the lost lamb, slinked from his home
among the dark and beautiful trees.

KING COMFORTER

When you leave me
in the morning, sleeping,
to make your tea
and write your poetry,
you must know
I slide to your side
and steal your body
pillow, holding it
in my arms
as if it were you.

Dear God, I love
your body pillow
almost as much
as I love your body,
which is sometimes
more than you
love your body—
O, lovely body!

Love, my love—
and now I mean
you—listen: I stripped
the bed this morning,
naked. Washed the sheets,
and dried them. And now,

as much of our bed
as I can make without you
I have made.

I need your help
to make the rest.

STARFISH IN THE MIDDLE OF THE BED

Today I found myself
alone in my own home
and rejoiced
because I am not usually,
nor do I usually seek to be.

This is the silence of steeping
tea, the science of watching trees—
the way the sun lights them
from top to bottom
as it rises over the ridge—
this is the first call
of the first bird
on the first morning
you are alone,
when you will not spend
your life this way.

I am in love and Love
is away for the day,
or for the night,
or even sometimes a week.
And I do not speak for days.

HAPPINESS ITSELF

Sometime after the vacation you deserved
but before the long weekend or the wedding
or the reunion you've been looking forward to—
and maybe dreading just a little—

but certainly between the love you made
and that made you both feel like newlyweds
and the dinner at the new restaurant
where you will stare into each other's eyes
like old lovers.

This is when it happens.

Reading in bed, when the night holds no surprises,
if you know where to look,
you may see Happiness itself,
or hear it, like the careful wind
sweeping through the quiet park nearby.

THE SPACE LONG-TERM LOVE REQUIRES

My wife and I are getting a new bed, a bigger bed, a king.
And everything arrived today—the frame, the two twin
extra-long box springs—everything. Everything except
for the mattress, which comes tomorrow. So tonight
we are sleeping for the last time on our old queen mattress
which lies in the middle of the vast new bed like an island,
the extra distance we will soon have between us visible now
in the gaps we each must cross to get to sleep.

But because I come to bed after a hot bath already sweating
and flushed, as though after making love, only to find Love
wrapped in the down comforter, freezing and not wanting me
to turn on the ceiling fan because, as she says, she is *friolenta*,
prone to coldness, I am here on the terrace off our bedroom, naked
in the early March night, cooling off and staring out at the moon
and the lighted clock of the Met Life Tower on Fourteenth Street.
It is probably safe to say we will not be having sex tonight.

Not with me standing naked on the terrace, standing in fact now
on one of the wooden patio chairs for all the midnight world to see,
steam rising from my body like prayers to the night, the moon,
the face of the clock, asking for more time to get this thing right
which has become my life, while my wife lies wrapped tightly
in goose down—big, thick, sexy wool socks on her feet—shivering
in the middle of a bed bordered on both sides by the same thing,
half the difference in inches between a queen and a king.

FOUR WAYS WE LOVE EACH OTHER

1. Falling in Different Directions

Because I think of falling in love as falling backward
and hoping my beloved will catch me, and you,
more like jumping off a cliff into the sea, your lover
at your side,

     I always end up with a concussion
or drowning when hoping for your hands, and you
break bones when I try to break your fall,
you expecting only water.

2. How the Family Factors into the Child's Idea of Love

Being an only child and needing,
perhaps, therefore more solitude,
you favor dropping me off
on abandoned street corners
at midnight and driving quickly away.

While I, middle child
of a large family, arms and legs
in every direction, lean more
toward the slow squeeze,
soft pillow of my love placed
over your nose and mouth

and held there until you stay
for good.

3. *You will never be alone*

is the last thing
you want to hear
but the only thing
I want you to say.

4. Loving Like Cats & Dogs

Love, to me, is a bounding dog,
all slobber and dependence and humping legs,
but for you, it is a cat, removed,
eyeing a songbird through the window;
for me it is a game of dress up we play each day,
but you, a stripping away, a midnight naked swim.

So we meet in the middle,
which is to say at twilight
in the bathtub to have sex
doggie style, you wearing nothing
but cat glasses, and me
singing softly, like a bird
outside the window, which,
of course, we leave open.

THE BLOOMING
(after Galway Kinnell)

Everything is a bloom, blessing many things
which then get called different names
because they blossom at unequal speeds,
like when it's quick and it happens in our heads
we call them ideas, and one can change the world.

And even life itself is only just the blooming
coming into flesh and living out the bursting.
But also the autumn is a kind of blossoming,
a softening and ripening, an understanding of the dark;
as is love, which is what we call it when it happens
in our secret startled hearts.

THE THING ITSELF

You will always be broke
if you have a job that pays you
at the end of every day in cash.
Any stripper will tell you this.

The key to the thing is not the thing itself;
there is the map, and there is the land.

Like when you think you're holding one
of your gloves in your other hand, also gloved—
that's when you are most likely to have lost it,
the one you thought you were holding,

which is now long gone and elsewhere,
your tightly fisted other gloved hand
having held nothing all this time
but itself, air, and maybe love,
the combination of which you took
to be something else entirely.

MONTREAL

I could tell in the way she kissed me
that she was bilingual.

There was a geography
in her lips I could taste

as if the muscles of her mouth
had known foreign tongues.

THE LOVING KILL
(for Bala and Jet Boy)

There on the floor
    (just between and before)
my wife and my clothes
    set out for the morning

lay a miniature crime scene:
    a mouse licked clean,
lifeless and still
    like a warning.

My wife makes a noise,
    I'm so proud of my boys!
They killed a mouse!
    Isn't that nice?

Meanwhile I'm thinking
    what has she been drinking?
Doesn't she realize
    this means we have mice!?

It just goes to show
    that you never know
what things with pride
    will fill you.

(And if you're a mouse,
     best stay out of this house.
'Cause we have two cats,
     and they'll kill you!)

READING ALLOWED

Maybe I met her in a restaurant.
Maybe I met her in a bar.
Maybe I saw her while stopped at a stoplight
driving down the street in my car.
And maybe it started out great,
like it does with every woman I've dated.
Amazingly passionate amorous love-making, totally caffeinated.
But no matter how varied our sex life,
eventually when we're in bed
women always ask me to do the same thing
and it's starting to mess with my head.

I feel I'm being used, maybe even abused.
I am trapped, and she is my captor.
She'll be naked, on her back, and she'll give me a look
and say, "I want you…to read another chapter!"

Women always want me to read to them.
They demand it. I have no choice
but to spread wide the pages of the book on the nightstand
and get busy giving good voice.
Because once upon a time we grew up on stories
and the voices in which they were told.
We need words to hold us, and the world to behold us
for us to truly know our souls.

So I read them *The Chronicles of Narnia*
and *The Education of Little Tree*,
and they close their eyes and listen, as I did
when these stories were read to me.
All of my siblings and all of our friends
(sometimes it was quite a crowd)
would gather and listen to my mom or dad
as they began to read aloud.

A different voice for every princess,
every knight and all the dragons.
When my mom read Tolkien you could tell the difference
between Frodo and Bilbo Baggins.

We spent so much time reading out loud
on long drives or nestled in reading nooks.
Much of the man I am today was influenced by all the
        good books
that my mother and father read to me when I was no more
        than a child.
I Know Why the Caged Bird Sings, and I know *The Call of the Wild*.
Charlotte's Web, Watership Down, Roll of Thunder, Hear My Cry,
The Diary of Anne Frank, A Wrinkle in Time, and *The King Must Die.*

Read to your children all the time:
novels and nursery rhymes, autobiographies,
even the newspaper. It doesn't matter, it's quality time.
Because once upon a time we grew up on stories
and the voices in which they were told.
We need words to hold us, and the world to behold us
for us to truly know our souls.

THE SEVEN DEADLY KAPPAS
(for the brothers and sisters of Kappa Psi Upsilon)

I tell my wife about The Seven Deadly Kappas, that list
of famous Biblical sins that appeared one morning
in permanent marker on the bathroom wall of my fraternity
revised so as to include with each sin the name
of one brother or sister in the house who seemed
to represent it best. The black ink always bled
to the surface every time it was painted over.

I tell my wife I was on that list and ask her to guess my sin,
thinking she might at first say Lust, but admitting secretly
she might just as easily say Gluttony, or Sloth; and never
guessing she would take my hand tenderly in hers and nail it,
saying, *You were Envy, weren't you?*

Immediately the shocked, hidden, indelible hurt wells up
again inside me. How could I be Envy? How could anyone
ever think I was Envy? How could I have carried these words
under my skin for all these years and not bled before now?

THE LAST TIME AS WE ARE

Because later that morning
　　the surgeon would cut me
four times, twice on each side,
　　once on the outside

and once on the inside,
　　leaving me with nothing
but tiny scars, and I would,
　　in a few months' time,

be able to be inside you
　　with nothing—not worry,
nor latex—I kissed you awake
　　when it was still dark,

and you opened to me,
　　and we made love
for the last time as we are,
　　as God made us,

which is to say,
　　as God made me.
Someday soon,
　　I will never be a father.

AS WITH A MARRIAGE AND ITS FIRE

I want to know if you will stand in the center
of the fire with me and not shrink back.
  —Oriah Mountain Dreamer

These blueberries get too much sun, I tell my wife as if I knew,
as if I were the earth from which these bushes grow, or one
of the very berries whose life it is to ripen, wither,
then drop off to feed the roots. *And these, too much shade.*

The nets have kept the birds away, and she works in silence,
wishing perhaps, I would as well.

But where the leaves of the bush itself have loosely thatched
the perfect mix of shade and sun, no one can deny the berries
there are fat and bursting in their blue. Yesterday we made love
twice, and for a time today in silence we pick berries for
  tomorrow's breakfast.

At this time of year we have to do this every day—
pick blueberries, the ones who seem to have ripened
after this morning's rain. And it doesn't sound, I know,
like as much of a chore as it actually is, as it can be
if you leave it until this late part of the afternoon,
or this hour of early evening, or you have worn shorts
and forgotten your hat, again.
Feeding the mosquitoes, it might as well be called.

One must stand inside the bush, I tell her, *and not shrink back,*
which I do believe. But I cannot help myself around this woman
whose silent ripeness I love, whose withering and
    dropping off
I will also love, so I add, *One must become the bush!* and she snorts
at my genius.

Soon enough it will be time to take away the nets and let the rest
of what we have but cannot use be eaten by the birds.
But as for now, come. We are enough.

REMEMBER ME FROM NOW

If for years before I die
I linger and wither
and forget myself,
like the old apple tree in the orchard
I cannot bring myself to fell;

if sadness or some other cancer
has spindled me to breaking;

then add that blue future
to the list of reasons
to remember me as I am now,
bursting in my glee,
in love with this day,
this forest, and these trees,
these dark and lovely trees.

STUDY QUESTIONS

1. The title of this collection of poems is also the title of one of the poems in the collection (see page 105). Is that an invitation to read that poem through a different kind of lens? How does the title inform the poem? Does it inform the book as a whole in the same way it informs the poem?

2. Consider the three sections of the book and the epigraphs that begin each section. Describe what you think the organizing principles were for deciding which poems went into each section. Does it really matter? How does the epigraph of each section inform that section? To what extent are all of the poems about teaching and learning?

3. Taylor Mali is fond of quoting the Latin poet Horace, who said that the task of the poet was to either instruct or entertain and that we must reserve our greatest approbation for those who do both at the same time. Do any of the poems in *The Last Time As We Are* seem as though they are **only** instructive or merely entertaining? Which poems do both most successfully? What do you think is more important: That a poem be instructive, or that it be entertaining?

4. Most poets will say they write for the ear, that their poems are meant to be read out loud, but Mali is a veteran of poetry slams, competitive poetry readings staged in bars and coffeehouses and judged by five random audience members. In fact, he refers to himself as a spoken word artist rather than a poet. In what poems can you see evidence of this background in performance? In what techniques or devices does that quality manifest itself most? Do they work as well on the page?

5. Does a poem have to be true? Does it have to be factually accurate? Is there a difference? The poem "The Moon, Exactly How It Is Tonight" suggests that sometimes it is necessary to add something that is not there in order to make an occurrence more believable. How is adding two feet to the height of Mt. Everest different from adding "two extra feet of moonlight" to an evening? In what other poems in *The Last Time As We Are* do you think Mali might be adding "two extra feet of moonlight"?

6. No one believes that poetry must necessarily follow all the grammatical rules that govern the writing of prose, and yet Mali's poems almost always do. They are, as Ezra Pound says all poems should be, "at *least* as well written as prose." There is a real fascination with the rules of grammar in *The Last Time As We Are*. Notice how many of the poems are only one or two sentences long. Pick a poem and discuss how Mali works with

and against the rules of grammar. Can syntax and grammar *keep* a poem from becoming too prosaic? Or does a rigid adherence to the rules of grammar work against a poem?

7. One of the criticisms most often leveled against spoken word poets who publish books is that their poems don't really work when read on the page. The specific complaint is that they don't know which word to end every line with. Mali has said he likes to break lines in such a way that a sentence says one thing when read *horizontally* (line by line) but another when read *vertically* (as a sentence). Find a few examples of where this might be true and discuss the extent to which the line break can be considered a form of punctuation.

8. How many of the poems in *The Last Time As We Are* rhyme? Considering that Taylor Mali has defined poetry as writing that is "honest, original, economical, and artful," how does his use of rhyme serve that definition?

9. The poem "Ars Poetica" (see page 45) mixes together many famous definitions of poetry that have been offered over the ages. Which ones do you think best describe Mali's own aesthetic? Consider specifically the idea that a poem can be a way to "rewrite history." Do you agree? Have you ever recounted a story from your own life in words or images that never occurred to you during the experience itself?

ABOUT THE AUTHOR

photo by Peter Dressel

Taylor Mali is one of the most well-known slam poets in the world. A former teacher and lifelong educator, he studied acting with members of The Royal Shakespeare Company and has put those dramatic skills to use performing and teaching poetry all over the world. He lives with his wife, the poet Marie-Elizabeth Mali, in New York City, where his family has lived since the early 17th century. When he is not traveling, Taylor Mali performs live every Tuesday night at the Bowery Poetry Club in New York City as part of the Urbana Poetry Slam.

OTHER GREAT WRITE BLOODY BOOKS

THE GOOD THINGS ABOUT AMERICA
An illustrated, un-cynical look at our American Landscape. Various authors.
Edited by Kevin Staniec and Derrick Brown

JUNKYARD GHOST REVIVAL
with Andrea Gibson, Buddy Wakefield, Anis Mojgani, Derrick Brown, Robbie Q,
Sonya Renee and Cristin O'keefe Aptowicz

THE LAST AMERICAN VALENTINE:
ILLUSTRATED POEMS TO SEDUCE AND DESTROY
24 authors, 12 illustrators team up for a collection of non-sappy love poetry
Edited by Derrick Brown

SOLOMON SPARROWS ELECTRIC WHALE REVIVAL
Poetry Compilation by Buddy Wakefield, Anis Mojgani, Derrick Brown, Dan
Leamen & Mike McGee

STEVE ABEE, GREAT BALLS OF FLOWERS (2009)
New Poems by Steve Abee

SCANDALABRA
New poetry compilation by Derrick Brown

I LOVE YOU IS BACK
Poetry compilation (2004-2006) by Derrick Brown

BORN IN THE YEAR OF THE BUTTERFLY KNIFE
Poetry anthology, 1994-2004 by Derrick Brown

DON'T SMELL THE FLOSS
New Short Fiction Pieces by Matty Byloos

THE CONSTANT VELOCITY OF TRAINS
New Poetry by Lea Deschenes

HEAVY LEAD BIRDSONG
New Poems by Ryler Dustin

UNCONTROLLED EXPERIMENTS IN FREEDOM
New Poems by Brian Ellis

LETTING MYSELF GO
Bizarre God Comedy & Wild Prose by Buzzy Enniss

CITY OF INSOMNIA
New Poetry by Victor D. Infante

WHAT IT IS, WHAT IT IS
Graphic Art Prose Concept book by Maust of Cold War Kids and author Paul Maziar

IN SEARCH OF MIDNIGHT: THE MIKE MCGEE HANDBOOK OF AWESOME
New Poems by Mike McGee

ANIMAL BALLISTICS
New Poetry compilation by Sarah Morgan

NO MORE POEMS ABOUT THE MOON
NON-Moon Poems by Michael Roberts

CAST YOUR EYES LIKE RIVERSTONES INTO THE EXQUISITE DARK
New Poems by Danny Sherrard

LIVE FOR A LIVING
New Poetry compilation by Buddy Wakefield

SOME THEY CAN'T CONTAIN
Classic Poetry compilation by Buddy Wakefield

COCK FIGHTERS, BULL RIDERS, AND OTHER SONS OF BITCHES (2009)
An experimental photographic odyssey by M. Wignall

THE WRONG MAN (2009)
Graphic Novel by Brandon Lyon & Derrick Brown

YOU BELONG EVERYWHERE (2009)
A memoir and how to guide for travelling artists by Derrick Brown with Joel Chmara, Buddy Wakefield, Marc Smith, Andrea Gibson, Sonya Renee, Anis Mojgani, Taylor Mali, Mike McGee & more.

WWW.WRITEBLOODY.COM

WRITEBLOODY
QUALITY AMERICAN BOOKS

PULL YOUR BOOKS UP BY THEIR BOOTSTRAPS

Write Bloody Publishing distributes and promotes great books of fiction, poetry and art every year. We are an independent press dedicated to quality literature and book design, with offices in LA and Nashville, TN.

Our employees are authors and artists so we call ourselves a family. Our design team comes from all over America: modern painters, photographers and rock album designers create book covers we're proud to be judged by.

We publish and promote 8-12 tour-savvy authors per year. We are grass-roots, D.I.Y., bootstrap believers. Pull up a good book and join the family. Support independent authors, artists and presses.

Visit us online:
writebloody.com